*Our Long Float*

# OUR LONG FLOAT

poems

Elizabeth Chapman

WHITE PINE PRESS / BUFFALO, NEW YORK

White Pine Press
P.O. Box 236
Buffalo, NY 14201

www.whitepine.org



Publication of this book was supported by public funds from the New York State Council on the Arts, with the support of Governor Kathy Hochul and the New York State Legislature, a State Agency.

Acknowledgments: See page 93

Cover Image: *Late Summer in Montana* by Matt Phillips.

Printed and bound in the United States of America.

ISBN 978-1-945680-91-5

Library of Congress Control Number: 2026934354

*For Katie*

CONTENTS

## MY GHOSTS, MY GUARDIANS



## OUR LONG FLOAT

NOW'S THE HONEY OF LATE SUMMER

# MY GHOSTS, MY GUARDIANS

## My Ghosts, My Guardians

*for the elephants of Botswana*

Not twenty meters from my lodge, there they are:
—massive, graywhite shapes, their ears swaying—
like benign shadows of our late beloveds.

I didn't hear them coming. Pads of fat and gristle
cushion their toes, and they walk without noise.

I think their silence is kindness. They breathe it out
the way trees transpire. Not visible, felt.
*Ubuntu*: I am because you are. I am because we are.

Today I wore the necklace my sister gave me long ago,
silvery, whose blue jewels flicker
through the lengthening spring evening.

She is very ill. Her husband says,
"I will not leave your side."

Note: Ubuntu: A Zulu word, part of a phrase that means, a person is a person through other people: an affirmation of humanity through one's recognition of an "other."

## For Dean Young

American Poet, 1955–2022

Here at altitude, dark of the moon,
my mind casts back to Africa this spring,
edge of the Kalahari, where the word for rain
is *pula,* the toast at peaches-and-blood
sundown is pu u u u la, —Let it rain—
and the word for connection is
*ubuntu:* I am, because you are.

In that harsh world, red-billed quelia flock
by the million, zebras thunder past by the hundred
and the elephants transpire kindness,
walking miles each day, pausing for the babies to rest,
just long enough, not too long.

Your journey on this earth is over.
A new heart carried you eleven years,
and here at altitude, dark of the moon
five years ago, when I was sick with grief,
you were crusty and gruff and you got me to laugh:
"Sometimes an indent can save your life."
Here's the bar, the table where we sat.
"Nothing funnier than the truth."
My ghost, my guardian. I come undone.

## Just off the dirt airstrip at Chobe

The dust is different here, holding
the scent of the rootedness of things.
A swoop a dive a lilac-breasted roller
perches on a mopane branch,
his colors speaking. And at night
the hippos grunt. The frogs clink.

Elephants, twenty or more, gather
at the river's edge, a mother
and her baby around three months old.
Her leg nudging under his belly
carefully she stabilizes him
and stretching out his small trunk
he drinks.

# Radiation Burn Cream

*for my sister*

Oil portion:
  calendula, sea buckthorn,
  cocoa butter, beeswax,
  essential oils of lavender, frankincense and myrrh.
Water portion:
  aloe vera juice,
  manuka honey.
Sea buckthorn, to improve blood circulation.
Humectant. I love the word, humectant.

A friend made this cream for you
while I was in Africa.
The dust is different there. Elemental.
The paths seem empty, but everyone
walks them, well trodden, packed hard.

If the body is dust, living and dying
in the same moment,
*Ubuntu* is the blood: A person is a person
through other people.

Long ago you gave me a necklace, blue gems
and twisted silver strands. I wear it
every day, in solidarity. You write
"Effects like fatigue and tender skin
are cumulative. Twenty treatments behind us,
seven to go. I feel well cared for and safe.
Eating is still very difficult, no
solid food."

## Botswana Farewell

This valley packed with life:
Dazzle of zebras
lioness at dawn,

leopard tortoise by the fence,
twenty pairs of hippo eyes
peering from the pond

and a fearful owl's single drawn-out note.
Now begins the dry time. The Delta
awaits her river, born high and icy

running down through Angola, through
Namibia, the panhandle,
shedding sediment,—

And luscious Okavango water
reaches the Delta wetlands, her
innumerable channels, the veins

of her body, till
at last absorbed by the sand
covering this earth, where we all began.

Goodbye, gray go-away bird,
incandescent waterlily light,
songs on my radio, ending often

with a drawn-out *Amen,*
then *Alleluia,* lifted and lilting.
The scent of 'oldest.'

## The Necessity of Milk, The Truth of Dreams, A Solstice

A Mozambique spitting cobra, slateblue and black:
our vehicle stops on the dirt road;
a second windshield pops up.

"No noise," our guide says; we know the creature is
malign—our shiver tells us. Our driver, steady and silent.
"They spray venom without flaring their hood,

several feet, cytotoxin, neurotoxin, through
pits in their front teeth, and it will
blind you."— a few yards from our bumper,

the creature glides off into grass and thornbush—
"unless....you must bathe the eyes.
Bathe them over and over, in milk."

***

Three things:
Hours later and last night
I dreamt of milk.
The San people, Baswara, call
the Milky Way *Backbone of Night.*
Exactly fifty years ago, my eldest child,
a girl, was born.

## Strawberry Moon

*For my sister Susan, in memory*

By the pond in their Vermont backyard,
grassy, full of June, three children are at play
beside the shallow water. Frogs, dragonflies, even
little turtles they dare each other to pick up.
Gravely ill, my sister wills herself downstairs
and out the back door, to watch. Their butterfly nets
catch nothing. Two boys, a girl; three, five, and nine,
shrieking, wading in the extra sand at water's edge—
trucked in— they call "the beach." Enough to dig
and excavate, yelling as loud as they want to, held,
intent and safe. This warm evening, late Spring.

# The Morning Air Is All Awash With Angels

— After Richard Wilbur

How could it not be?
Late June, the high Sierra, the creek
you'll hear before you see,
the water running swift and clear.
Add boulders, all sizes, round, cracked,
rough edges, sharp
and wade in
far enough so the cold, nearly ice,
grips your ankles.
Make an offering: a couple bills fall
from your unzipped pocket,
eddying away.
Add one gray water ouzel, dipping
and industrious, swimming his streamline.
Sit on a rock,
try to catch a glimpse of his white
eyelid feather,
and when he flies around a curve
right past you, stand up
and lose your balance,
and scrape your shin.
Breathe in, the air is still awash with angels,
and the ouzel feathers you.
Ashore, grab a bunch of white yarrow,
flower and leaf. Lightly crush them,
press against the bleeding place.
Hold them there.

# The Music of What Happened: December 31, 1943

Their flat on Commonwealth Avenue so small,
a string tied to their bedpost would rock
the cradle in the next room.

The war; rationing; my father
 publishing urgent appeals—*Flatten Your Tin Cans,*
*Buy U.S. Savings Bonds*—in one-act plays for children.

A pram hulking in the damp hallway, pigeon-gray.
My mother, more beautiful than she knew,
bemoaned her breast-size, kerchiefed her dark blond hair.

They were outgoing, they were hospitable,
inviting lots of folks— nearly everyone they knew—
for New Year's Eve.

Coffee brewing, from the A & P with the huge
grinder in the middle of its wooden floor.
Two kinds of crackers: the square ones,

Saltines, and the ones born at the height
of the Great Depression, Ritz. And cream cheese.
They made merry. They lived within their means.

I will tell you what he told us
  clustering around him in the foyer
of the old convent *Posada de las Monjas*
  the smell of good coffee and the smoky fire
and the sweet round of Epiphany bread
  circling the room *All poetry comes from*
*listening to what you don't know*
  *you're listening to* he said stretching out
slim legs in jeans cowboy boots
  with curved tops their pattern finely traced
He took questions *Who is the dreamer*
  someone asked how does that process work
That's what you spend your whole life
  finding out He might deny this but by then
we could have been any age
  sitting on the floor roughly an oval
absorbing him as later
  the children of the town would the *Reyes Magos*
with their spices and bronzefoil coins
  Tell us your best secrets
Poetry is about relation what cannot be said
  Read us a poem and tell us why you love it
From his chambray shirt pocket a sheet of paper
  Write some out to carry when you travel
Do you know Hardy's *Proud Songsters?*

*The thrushes sing as the sun is going,*
*And the finches whistle in ones and pairs*
*...As if all time were theirs...*
*A year ago or less than twain*
*No finches were... But only*
*particles of grain*
*And wind, and earth, and rain*

This is an image of everything he said
  the silver hair the still immensely clear

blue eyes  You sing and you won't
    be there after awhile
Do I have to tell you why I love that poem
    All you have is the sound of the bird

## Hexham Abbey on a March Night

Dark settles on the shoulders of this town,
the scent of rain. I walk downhill from my friends' house.
The names of Anglo-Saxon saints spilling
off the chapel wall: Athelbert, Egbert, Ethelbert, Wilfred.
Maybe a dozen of us for Evensong, this nearly-spring
evening. The words rise, beautiful as ever—
*Now lettest thou thy servant depart in peace....*
*Defend us from all perils and dangers of this night*—
from the small red prayer book, firmly stamped
Not To Be Taken Away. I turn to leave, and there's a tug
at my elbow, the verger. Solid, creaky of gait,
giving back the book, "You're not from here.
Take this with you." His voice redolent of the North's
generous heart. Briefly I think of the scones we had
for tea: warm, large, slightly misshapen, fragrant.

## Blizzard

*for my mother*

A horse runs past me
silent silent at her burial
in seas of snow.
Her words slide out
as cold thread.
*Please do not forget me.*

# The Muse You Were

She can pick them out in the dark:
Leo, Draco, the Lynx, the Double Cluster,
 a very few delicate constellations.

She'll reveal three things she's kept:
            The highball glass stamped "Happy,"
            The key ring, very solid, very Topeka
                        very Menninger's, where he trained,
            The pewter mug for pens,
when people ask,
Do you find yourself thinking of him?

Many years gone now,
the spouse, the muse, the good doctor,
and going, long
before that, going.

It's dangerous,
this opening wide to small stings.

She doesn't say aloud
  Before I die
  I'll be able to think of him whole,
  walking, warm.  But not yet.

Before the multiple sclerosis quite
ravaged him,
when she was writing, sleepless, stuck
in the night,
he would say,

*Go back to the first draft, Sweetheart,*
*everything you need is there.*

That was his true voice, a plumb line.

## Earth Day Ramble

The Paschal moon and her lava-filled seas
are watching
the Lyrid meteors falling from the night sky,
a comet's bits and pieces.
Can she forgive all this fracturing? Can we?

☆

She's also called Pink Moon, from a flower,
the moss pink, or, creeping phlox.
And I find myself thinking of my father,
the pride he took in his rock garden,
sweet alyssum, begonias, greened boulders,
and his tender pruning of cherry trees, till they broke
from the weight of an April ice storm.

☆

He wasn't perfect, but what he was, was
patient.
Forgiveness is another name for Spring.
And the thing to trust, is roots.

☆

Did you ever have something you planted
entirely dug up?
Whether or not you know
everything about lonely old ladies,
replanted,
even if you're just beginning to sow
those field peas, and hard-working oats,—

☆

The silent moon looks down. The bees
are eternally attracted
as, in their storm-shaken boughs,
the birds are sleeping.

# By An Ancient Fishing Pond, Kaupulehu, Hawaii

It seizes you
and casts a guava spell
this night before the new moon
the invisible one
Now the blue whales pass by
departing for Alaska singing
their invisible songs

The unseen turtles are foraging
in their strong shells warmed
all afternoon beneath a tradewind sky
The wild donkeys have left behind
their rusted bray
that rose from the black
lava caves and mesquite thorns

It binds you
like a language you love
but do not fully understand
this waking in the Kona dark
What was left unfinished
righted here  It smells like
coconut like coffee

*Ho'o mená venúi*  Slow down
If departure is the great truth
arriving is better beginnings are better
Now the francolins start
their morning racket in the trees
spring tides swell the lagoon
and the palms drink

## Stella

*for my daughter's daughter*

We're on a far shore
near the manta ray's rock
where she folds
and unfolds herself
The stars burst forth
Before the bright hotel was built
the Southern Cross
glowed visible

April in three weeks
you'll more or less swim
yourself out from the darkness
that still flecks the iris
of your eyes like black salt
from Molokai

The astronomer
loops the naked Pleaides
and through his lens
we can glimpse hidden
as you are still
hidden the cloud
of your bright burning

If I knew how to paint
a guardian spirit
I'd brush an *ama kua*
right on your crib
a *honu* in Pacific green
who would hear
every sob and quirk of you

There's a gate at home
missing a latch
I've left it open

One day when you come
seeking riding through

the miles of night
holding on to Leo's
generous mane
I will wait for you
Stella by starlight

Note:

*Ama kua* divine spirit
*honu* sea turtle

# Hanalei

All week catching sight of the green steepness
   and diamond taro fields since plucking up
the fruit that fell in front of me on the trail
   near Ke'e deciding to bite through its gold coat
tasting the pulp and sacs of juice that keep the heft
   of pollen and smelling all week that tart and silken
lilikoi while the house on Weke and the birds
   in their hedge went quiet in the heat's long sigh
swimming in their own current I was lapsing
   into the Old Style green paint the seams obvious
hearing the *nene* call their way to night
   *na aina kai* their names coming in clear
through the thin roof while the ceiling fan
   echoing some farther sea brushed my shoulders
hush hush hush sending its persuading breath
   inside the arc of rib that hollow place
you never think about back of the heart
   All through that long week by the last day
I realized everywhere else I've been homesick
   for here One hundred yards away a blue tarp
folds over the outrigger and at six
   the sunset men put out their war canoe
arrowing it straight-armed toward the pier
   On this long sand at Wa'ipo someone's always
getting married as the year's turning
   Do you trust the spendthrift tide sweet beach

# The Day is the Island

and the island a man who loves you
hearing the ubiquitous chickens of Kauai
uncaged since Iniki wrenched them free
The rooster will begin at dawn

who loves you
setting a green chair under the ironwood tree
and drinking coffee there
The campfires have gone out

and the tide going out too He loves you
while you wait in the coconut wind for dawn
to complicate things

# OUR LONG FLOAT

## Our Long Float

*for Matt*

Our long float:
the two of us
sneaking out the back door
of the world,
from the names of towns,
Fishtail and Columbus,
once Eagle's Nest, once Sheep Dip,
past the stone one-room schoolhouse,
our Jeep with torn seats
pointing to the Beartooth's jawline,
now sliding one leg over
the raft's rubber edge,
the other, sunk
in the Upper Stillwater.
There's no word for the sound
of this white foam,
this bouldery back-and-forth,
the spill of blue cold,
the oarlocks' creaking.
What's intimate is never still.
You get to hold a rainbow's
firm wet flesh, his orange gill-plate,
his showering colors
flipping till he's freed
into his own depth and speed.
This air
haloing the river
tastes like granite.

## In Arcadia

Far from the tremor and shift of tides,
looking up, dark-adapted, she can find Pegasus' great

square body, pacing beside the North Star,
plowing silent as the ends of bones.
Creek-cleaned, huckleberry-oak-dusted, a few notes

of *Redemption Song* from someone's car nearly dissolve her,
recalling her godmother, now late, how she sat

in her ancient mariner's cap of navy wool,
reading the tea leaves: "The lifeline's there,
not broken. You are two in one; it's the fusion that I see."

Your letter arrived today, a surprise snapshot
of Pray, Montana, the house and studio you built

nearly dissolving in sunset light.
"When you come it'll be goddam hot." And,
quoting Milton Avery, "Why talk when you can paint?"

You'll stand in the river, casting.
I'll sit on the bank with a basket of fruit, and write.

## "Wide, Bold, Rapid and Deep:"
## Banks of the Yellowstone, Livingston, Montana

As you give me facts
about fish,
the current braids
and rebraids itself over the rocks.
"Fish feed in the riffles
under a pocket of water....
They have a memory, if they've been hooked."
The clouds are rough boulders.
An Absarokan wind
lifts everything today, so clear
the sun's ringing off the trees,
an axe cleaving ash wood, baring
its blue heart.
"Another thing: We do not discuss
missed fish."

## Reading the Water, Mending the Line

A lone hopper cried in the sweet grass of morning.
A bald eagle draped his soaked wings.
Rowing, our guide spoke softly:
*I want you casting there, in that backwater.*
*Two more inches.* The line bowed.
*A nice little cutty,* he said, showing me
the two orange slashes at the throat.
"There's more to fishing than catching fish",
you often say, "But a fish wouldn't hurt."

Here, where the river narrows most,
just past a slump of half-picked buffalo bones,
a rapid dropped our boat—
the bow rising, my red notebook swimming,
the guide's knife poised to cut the anchor rope—and
the snag relented. Righting us, he told you, *Give 'er a mend.*
And you throw a loop in the last summer air.
Slowing the fly imparts a natural drift:
The trouts' curve, the river, curving us,
we three bending to it.

## House on Yellowstone Trail

There will be plenty of dark to pray in, very soon.
Beyond our ken, the eyes of animals search the dusk.
I grab the sack of wild birdseed we picked up in Emigrant—
it's opened, spilling over—and, squinting at the plan
the builder left, throw a handful, then another at the base
of each new tree. Poplar, cottonwood, chokecherry.
Blue spruce. A sudden gust clatters the chairs on the porch;
trails of seed, like gold beads, like exotic roe, diffuse.
You're still working in the studio to steal the last light:
a hover of trout, a grist of bees, a husk of hares
incandescing in the prints on the etching press.
The air is moist, sticky, a dough. Tonight it will rain.

# Couple

Lemon verbena leaves in a glass pot
steeping and the steam rising up
the scent of vegetable & mineral
all the little things
nobody else knows about

## There Had Been a Prolonged Drought

The night breathed around us
one hummingbird sipped his way
from well to cobalt blue well
salvia conspiring with coconut thyme
white lavender and the calm air
receiving it smells wonderful here
he said some things you don't forget
like crickets' undertow when they come
back each summer we went inside
what needed to burn quickly did
touch cleaned us everything we were
was touch and absolved us became our
breathing a quiet lake the shore

## Cases of Magic

populate the long room, like a ship's deck,
with a rare wedding cape at the end:
Kilims and photos of Montana sky
—portfolios of cloud—
tophat and jugglers' balls the least of it.
                    There were live doves too,
                    till a weasel ate them.

Dozens of framed monotypes, small beauties
resembling the ones you gave me.
All flowers, pressed on rice paper
with a tablespoon. The whispered look of them.

*Love notes*
*Practice sketches*
*Summer madness*
*Made for you*

The only flaw is time, and our ages.

I trust you.  Do you trust me?

*I trust you the way I trust those peonies*
*in the Belleek vase and I will call you*
*something out of Science of the Night,*
*my careless sprawler.*

Above the table, the lamp's  a soft inverted cone.

Did you know, fireflies flash
only in the last two months of their life?

*Well, I will bring you coffee on a tray*
*in the morning and lift the shade*
*you never open, one-fifth of the way,*
*for the cherry tree light to fall in on us.*

# Spring Meant Ranunculus

Bright yellow, often.
"Why are you so afraid
of color?" he'd say—
a vase half-filled, the leaves stripped off:
"I like them in their underwear."

# Magician, Age Eight

"A bulb would light up
in my room when my mother's
foot reached the top step."
Upstairs, a thin wire
lurked beneath the hall carpet.
An early gift for misdirection.

# Eclectic Breakfast at the MT Cup

"Bagel and lox and cream cheese…"
    And to drink, Sir?
"…a light cappuccino."
You're at the window table. The whole
September day stretches forward.

## “I Raised Thee Up Under an Apple Tree”

*The Song of Solomon*

Eve unashamed
unfolds and reveals
her bluish skin

Paired red apples
spots of blood
float overhead

I am the Rose of Sharon
this evening
flattened with heat

## Recipe for a Monotype

"Petals, flowers, leaves,
painted on Japan paper
and pressed with a spoon."
Nature, or Art? "Both.
Plus a bit of experience."

# Dark Night, Edge of the Trail

"It can be lonely here...
What if someone tries to break in?"

You could tack a sign to the front door:
*Mauvais Chien*

"I see. For the educated marauders."

## At Present

We picked up cold soup, cucumber mint,
from the Mustang Café in Livingston and now

walk down your road twenty minutes or so
till you tire—as far as the watering tanks

for your neighbor's small flock of Jacob sheep.
An ancient breed, going back to the Bible,

prized for their horns and pied fleece.
My fake baa-ing doesn't fool them.

Between hayings seems a season all its own:
The bales, neatly rolled green cylinders, fill

the valley where we saw the sandhill cranes,
eager in the feeding-fields, their plumage stained,

humbled by the river mud they preen with.
You fret about the cottonwood that died

and a reflector light the wind blew over.
I plan to surprise you with a bluebird box

for your birthday in a week. Nailed tight
to its post, empty until March.

Two deer, doe and fawn, blossom out of nowhere.
Soon, you're musing over the soup: "Excellent,

in two years, these folks could cater a big
birthday party, right here." Honey. Don't wait.

## Dusking

And always downhill the white horse
paces, tail swishing, muzzle to foreleg,
whickers good evening to the farrier's mare
grazing close to the river whose tides
we are powerless to control.
Deep-fingered wings
live alongside us.
Will this be the last summer? The last
rabbit we find, crouched under the doorstep
each still-chilly morning? Late bellman, pale
heart-shape face, patrolling the harrowed field:
You have me in your sights, barn owl.

## Providence

At Mallards' Rest the fishing
access off Highway 89
near Pray, we pulled in
so I could chill
my swollen stitched foot
in the Yellowstone.
A family was camping
noisily there a radio
blaring two six-packs
Fritos and two kids,
their truck at the edge
where the bank was steep.

Inching down, I clung to the roots of trees.
A voice behind me said,
"Let me help you.
I know just what surgery
you had. Give me that arm."
And holding firmly,
her bikinied and tattooed body
supported my tilting
shoulder and hip.
She continued, "The kids were small
and I scooted around the house
on my bottom for six months
with my leg in the air."
We sat on flat rocks
under the old cottonwoods
exactly where Lewis and Clark
soaked their horses' bruised feet.
"Look," she said showing her
tanned foot with its toe rings
and berried nails,
then with a half fireman's carry

pulled me back up
through the muddy spot.
"You'll be fine. It'll take a year,"
and she was right.

Today in the high meadow
I can close my eyes and see my benefactress
her face a kind cloud
suffused with the sunset light
my friend called a crack in the world

# Fifi L'Amour and Jean-Paul Sartre en France

"I need silence!" You tuck yourself in,
then I start laughing. Then we can't stop.

There are absurdities: Across the street
from our hotel, Berkeley Books of Paris,
and, at L'Opéra, an Apple Store.

Next day, your cell phone call:
"I wish to be connected to the Wells Fargo Bank."
An eternity of clicks. *Monsieur,*
*you've reached the Fire Department of France.*

It made as much sense as
tidings of magpies
in the chestnut trees.

The river's a sleek animal.

There's time for one museum, so I defer to you,
the painter. Without pausing, "Monet."

Inside the great oval, *Les Nymphéas,* the light
is the light that has bedded down
with darkness, has known the galled depths of war:

Grass light, lilypad light, a lilac tide
without horizon.

We stand silent, tiny surprises
all the time, hints of forest, brief
passages of entry.

The long wave we don't want to end.

Like holding onto a string of pearls
when you've removed it,
lighter, somehow, in your hand,
and warmer for the weight of where it's been.

Hot milk makes coffee more forgiving.

You've stuck a Post-it in my notebook:
*Tout est possible, Fifi.*

## Sarlat, The Market

Even in rain watching it unfold
just down the alley from the churchyard plums
two sorts of umbrellas opening
over vegetables and customers whose sacks
and baskets overflow as if the bison's eye
from yesterday's cave had followed us back
Is there one past or many  The old man next door
can remember when the Germans found him
then a teen and the pack of cigarettes
in his pocket which he gave them and they
went off up the honeystone street
in a cold breeze  Today another wind
blows through this town of bells and books and vines
Still he can make his way downhill
to the Saturday market to the fraises
the wild red berries at its heart
All the little renaissances of the day

Either we've always lived here
or haven't quite arrived
Two ladies in dark dresses point
delicately to the muguet des bois
nodding in glass jars lily of the valley
whose fragrance means love requited
as we're leaving with our bouquets
a young man calls out, "Like this,"
holding out his hands dirt creasing his palms
abiding in those lines he harrows and sows
*a la méthode ancienne* linden and lime blossom
for the *tisane* he's named *Douce Nuit*
a small pinch between thumb and forefinger
he promises us a bowl of sweet night
all of a sudden we smell earth  Like this

## Fidèles

I'll remember the poplar drift
on April's river, the air thick
with seeds on long soft hairs,
thistles without sting
parachuting down and all around
the *bateau promenade*
sailing downstream the easy way
to Bordeaux.

Five hundred years old, our hostelry
at 9 Rue Montaigne was standing here
when Shakespeare was alive.
Rutted stone steps.
Huge iron key. An ancient lock
we fumble with, every night.

Two reindeer in the constant air
at Font-de-Gaume,
facing one another: The way she kneels,
her small horns beneath
his muzzle, while he sniffs
at her head. The way his antlers
define the painted scene— blown through
bones, blown from human mouths—
peace. Not one animal is killed.
Inside this place, there is no war.

At Le Glacier, the café where
we go most nights fot supper,
something simple with salad and *frites,*
it's balmy and we eat outdoors in the lengthening
evenings. The owners, by the fifth time,
call us *"Les Fidèles,"* and bring an ice cream
with a pinwheel on it.

At La Lanterne, our *chambre d'hôte,*
there is time, for the courtyard in shade,
the chaffinch call at dusk,
this ivy, this limestone wall,
this scarlet geranium.
And tomorrow on the ledge
outside our bathroom window,
having once more hauled himself up
five floors into spring, there will be
one plain, brown, skinny lizard of Sarlat.

# NOW'S THE HONEY OF LATE SUMMER

Now's the honey of late summer,

asters and salvia. It's darker, and the sunset light
fully illuminates your photo on my bookshelf,
the lily-of-the-valley stems you hold
against your broad lapel.
In the Dark Perigord it was Springtime—
We'd been watching the early market
come to life.

Back from Montana
just now, I'm absorbing the layers Kunitz tells us
to live in. Well-weathered brick
of the bars along Second and Main
the Owl, the Mint, the Whiskey;
the whistle of a train reaching through the night
is the sound of longing, a longing
released just now when I sent our broadside—

my next-but-one copy— to our guide,
your deep friend, just now fallen in love.
He wants to show her how it felt that day
on the Stillwater, the sky achingly blue
and the clouds' striation, proof
that September's the best month in Montana.

I fold the kitikata Japanpaper you preferred
around your animated fisherman stirring the air
around my poem longish
and skinny and around our guide's
voice, his oars, his wisdom—
"You have to have a feeling for good water."
all of it, layering.

Sealing the padded envelope, handing it
to the postmistress felt almost as if
you were dying all over again,—
Then a half-smile
realizing, recognizing that our tiff
the day we were flying back
wasn't really about locating the UPS store
(backseat piled with paintings to send after us)
nor my needing lunch, nor forgetting
to turn off at the dump,
nor the rain wetting and tiring
us both. None of that.

Instead, the deep-buried knowledge,—
This was the finish,
the last time we'd be there together
with the wind through the alders,
those long shadows on Yellowstone Trail,
the view from your kitchen window
including the Crazies, the laughter,
the mystery.

# Midnight Exhibition at the Wheatgrass Saloon

When the sky's elderberry dark like this
I will go back to that evening up the steep
flight of stairs and the green velvet couch
where you held court and barely sipped the Scotch
you'd asked for and the townfolk came round the magic
in the paintings though the Las Vegas photos
neon and chorus girls did mildly shock them
when they'd all left and we walked hand in hand
through the sleet down the alley of September
I will go back and it will pierce me your bright blue
shirt the silver belt buckle full cowboy attire
including the forest green beaver hat
and horsehair band you wore the turquoise ring
bejewelling the night and the wind that
never quite leaves Paradise Valley it will
blow the door off your car if opened carelessly

## God's Spies

"And take on's the mystery of things"
—Shakespeare, *King Lear,* Act V

Here's Aries the Ram,
well up in the East right now,
a rectangle with two chunks
missing from the corners.
Allow me to imagine us
rejoined, as if seeing everything
from another place,
looking down the far coast
where seals haul out
to sun themselves and pup.
There we are, downtown— both of us
born into winters where snow
came in sideways, drifting, shawling—
There we are, stepping inside
Café Zola's bright stripe of life,
our table close to the kitchen,
our small tub of black-olive butter.
Tearing off a crust
you're leaning forward:
"Let me tell you something."

## Magpie, Redux and Sorrow

The fence stretches edge to edge
casting blue shadows on the snow.
Perched on the gate, he draws the eye—
his dark head and thickish body
far left of center, exactly as
Claude Monet has left him, gracing
the beholder, that winter light
and, last year, my greeting card.
As he will this year, too. Here, white
pelicans, returning hungry, alive,
dip their beaks in brackish tide—
that is our marshland's beauty.
But I will go back to the painted image,
its somber bark and iced branches,
to the magpie—his black
cloak. It is consoling me still.

## Winter Song

Never mind now past gardens inhabit us
the trenched asparagus and elongated marrows

my weeping purple copper beech what if our life
were an unpunctuated sentence branching leaf-

furnished or bare your cherry tree's gray pitted bark
framing the upstairs casement window it comes back

to gardens before words a delphinium's blue eye
to a hummingbird's winged vibration beyond light

## My Other Life

At last I can stop my jailbreak song
and dance, leave a life as solitary
as those nesting bees, whose shelter is holes,
not hives, who make no honey.

The best day, you always said, is the day
you arrive.
            and this year, my first minute
            in the airport lobby, glimpsing
            the bronze grizzly—"Guardian Spirit"—
            I was free.

Same with your son, driving west with his family,
who camped near Normal, Illinois one night,
on the edge of a lavender field
with a view of infinite plains.

A poor dissembler, I'd told no one my plan
and my first walk to the river scares me,
till, on Yellowstone Street, I see the magpies
gorging on bright orange chokecherries—
Did you know, three or more can be
a tiding?

I know that here I will be fed.
Coyotes of the sky, these birds
cackle and strut and steal,
and when one of them dies,
perform an elaborate ritual of grief.

"One for sorrow, two for joy," in their
phosporescent purple plumage, especially
when this falling equinoctial light catches them
sideways, they are beautiful. They feel what happens.

Red staghorn sumac shades the garden on your birthday.

And now from the rooftop patio,
the signs are visible:  Owl Lounge,
the Mint Bar,  "Terminator" at the Odeon,
all in neon under a cloudridden moon

in this very old hotel, right up against the rail depot.
Freight arrives throughout the night.
Three blasts of the whistle, every single time.

## The Moon Is Down

I catch myself thinking,
I should write and tell him
his poplars got through the winter,
or that the bluebirds are back.

## Life Raft

What if God
were the friends
keeping my head
above water now
barely afloat

# The Things You Say You'll Never Do—Until You Do Them

Twenty-three years ago, my handsome husband far gone
down the unrelenting road that is MS,
finding myself unable to write—at all—I came to
this high Sierra valley, not skeptical so much as scared
in my prim but not unbecoming Laura Ashley dress,
legal pads and fountain pens. On Wednesday, I wrote
about him—tacking like a toddler across the house
exposed, a crustacean with no shell, and out of nowhere
came the words, "There's no explaining attachment—
nor how, by being loved, we're loveable." There,
in the Buckter House living room, Galway Kinnell read
those lines back to me, squashed on the sofa. Life
was never the same again.

In 2008, widowed then, I broke my own rule (Never
answer a personal ad) on a stormy night, in fact
Valentine's Day, wind shaking my tiny bungalow, read,
"East Bay painter and printmaker ISO woman with brains
and a funnybone." As if disconnected from my brain,
cold fingers replied (water dripping through the borderline
roof), "Palo Alto poet loves Shakespeare
and bubblebath." We had ten years, nearly, nearly
effing perfect as my daughters would say, including
once, right here, mail arrived from him (real mail),
a list of twelve jazz tunes, woven into monotypes,
from "Lucky to be Me" to "There'll Never Be Another You."
They became a book, *All That Jazz.*

Yesterday, walking in bright sun, I made my usual
pilgrimage to the creek, saw a water ouzel browsing
the stream, imagined the nictating membrane sealing
his eyes, never too cold out to interrupt his finding
food. And last night at the reading, under snow-patched
shale slopes, the peak, and the pinkie-finger new moon,

frog-speak and cricket-speak, hearing our poets,
I was shivering, glued to my seat.  And from nowhere, a hand
dropped a warm red blanket on my lap.  "You saved me,"
I spoke into the dark, and that, that is community—
I could stay to the end, and was grateful.

## A Season of His Own

The new moon's sliver of hope
rises into August, your birth month,

the grass tawny-silver with it.

> "There are a lot of mysterious things around here,
> and that includes us."

A blue dusk falls, and out of nowhere,
a towhee's frilled call

hovering.   My Leo, my cranky charmer.

## Cloud Effects

"Things look different on the water
including clouds and their shadows.
They amuse the eyes."

River, cloud, eyes—
their aqueous humor, their vitreous humor—
whose irises'
brown depths hold all

the mystery of a forest, a cloud,
a keepsake. All those times
you'd pull over,

stop the car
and, in a wailing Absorokan wind,
point your camera at the sky.

## A Great Profusion, the Clematis Like Purple Stars

Remember the summer evening voices
you took with you into the dark

Simple as bacon and eggs or a brown trout
nosing the surface

Your neighbors the Chicory Gang
together on this shelf above the river

Burnt smell in the air a campfire at Pine Creek
bigger fires elsewhere here's your voice

"If there's a gathering after I'm gone, I can tell you this:
I won't be there"

> Oh yes you are.
> Take my hand.

So often those long days of heat and haze
and chatter you'd say "Will you just stop talkin'?"

> *Do you love an apple?*
> *Do you love a pear?*
> *Do you love a laddie*
> *With curly brown hair?*

The song falling in this twilight a spark
feeling that thump on your line
          you set the hook

> *Oh but I still love him*
> *I can't deny him*
> *I will go with him*
> *Wherever he goes*

Round bales in fields along the road
          Where did you come from
my first dream of fishing this carrying breeze

*Prunus virginiana demissa*

Even now
the trout rise
reaching toward their future
it is the warming of things
ripples of you
reverberate along the river
and today a red cherry tree
was planted in your honor
may it grow hardy
and generous of blossom

Note on the title: *Prunus....*The Latin botanical description for the Canada Red Cherry, also known as Western Chokecherry.

# This Hour of Limestone Light

We've been tallying bald eagles
and we're at five, a true convocation,
mustering on the east wind.
Just two of us today, the guide and me
floating downriver, when we come to a sign,
hand-lettered, CAUTION: Wrecked Raft
at Beartooth Drop, and its twisted frame
abandoned on the far bank,
like a mattress at the dump, which is how we learn
that the old way of navigating will not work now;
so, on the diagonal, then sideways
and back a little, we maneuver to the edge
tasting whitewater, a roaring, and we're down.
Peace falls upon us, the ospreys
and mergansers, coexisting there.
*I'm going to catch one for Matt.*
He's putting on waders, jumping out
in the shallows, and soon, here's a brown trout,
smallish, whose scales, overlapping, become
the minutes, the seconds, the past.
It's like nothing else.
What would I give for one more day,
just you and me beside the river,
and the chairs set up for lunch?
You don't need me to tell you that.
Ask the cottonwoods, rustling.
Ask the Stillwater.

# I Call It Deep Pool

The last painting you made for me,
its blues so saturate, the paper nearly sodden,
I imagine it still damp to the touch.
No time for a formal border, you
sketched the interrupted black lines of one
whose breathing came, often, staggered then.

What do I call the place I'm in,
its weather? the weather of it,
the cold wet fog or heavy mist?
In Suffolk, maybe, "sea-fret."
                    I do love a spondee.

I'm still finding Post-its you'd hide
when I was out of the room:
"Against all odds, I find I still love you."
Who else in the world would print
on a bright blue square, "Tout est possible, Fifi,"

and paste it to my notebook?
People said, "He was old." Why, yes he was.

I hear that some familiar birds of summer
are disappearing now, their cries few and faint
that once were numerous among the meadow hay.
          Corncrake. Crex crex. Nightjar.

# Blue Valentine

I wake to midsummer sky, clear
and flawless, a pearl, the air
thin and cool. I want to wear it.

*

Your son's summarily dispatched
the nurse I call the death angel,
tasked with sending you—where, exactly?—
who's been roosting by the door, in her black
scrubs. I want to rip them off her,
embodying a true unkindness
of ravens. I'm a wolverine.
They can take down an elk. Tree a bear.
Not a question of size—smallish—
but, all attitude.

And, out of nowhere
as he steps away, your son is quoting Yeats:
"Once more the storm is howling,
and half hid..." Just the worst
weather of the year, February rain
smacking the hospital window,
hour upon hour. You know you're safe
for now. Here, my love, a card for you:
Midnight and deep cerulean, strung
with a necklace of glitter-stars.

The ruffle of a heart.
Your hands, always warmer than mine,
stroking my wrist, now, your fingers so dry.
"A sonnet, OK?" I ask, pulling up a chair,
right side, your good ear. Tiny nod.
"When in disgrace with fortune..."
until at heavens gate, my voice cracks.

"Don't cry." A fluttering, a blink
and your painter's eye opens.
"You look good in pearls."

## Finding You

MP,

Love lies where it falls.
Fifteen months since you died.
I don't know what happens
after death, but you sure
visit me a lot. I dreamed
we were at one of the bars
here in Tahoe, sharing
a weak "Chicotini:" vodka,
Clamato, and —the secret—
a small cloud of pepperoncini
juice. Here's my promise for
when I'm propelled off
this planet: Energy is never
lost, in this universe,
so I will find you, wherever
you and your spirit
happen to be hanging out.
Your arms will be strong as ever,
and I will wrap mine around you,
careful not to squeeze
your bad shoulder. Where there's
no natural light, our interiors
will be lit
EXCLUSIVELY by 100-Watt
incandescent light bulbs
that I will go to jail, if need be,
to protect and preserve.
Kind of nutty, right? But
you always said I'm the nuttiest
woman you ever met. Remember

the Paddington books we got

at Hatchards for your grandson?
I won't appear as a bear
from darkest Peru, but might wear
a label:  Please look after this
human.  No marmalade required.
One more thing: for the nights
when you go to sleep and I cannot,
I'll bring plenty of murder mysteries.
We'll always come back to laughter.

E

# A Thirst

I dreamed that I collided with a river, and
the river was angry.

The house on Yellowstone Trail
sleeps on towards August.
At Mallards' Rest, awash,

no patch of earth is visible.
Last year, poor-boxes collected alms
for the drought-dried trees

whose shadows give comfort
and safety to the trout: willow,
alder, poplar, aspen,

mountain ash, whose roots
are busily drinking now. And still
it rains. I won't drink the river,

but assuredly I'll drink it in
like swallowing starlight
made blue by darkened dust—

the embedded stars of Cygnus.
And here's memory, whose arms
spread wide like your small grandson's

last September, out on the deck;
Labor Day; the barbeque.
"GrandMatt would've loved this."

I see you everywhere. He has your eyebrows.

## In Which I Take Heart

Things unclog here.  Adrenalin rises, the blood
is rising and at night, over the clear outline
of the crematorium and its smokestack,
so is a waning, gibbous moon,
readying for the equinox.

It's straightforward:  The hops lace their trellis,
tomatoes sweeten and the slowed,
warmed river takes her course eastward
toward the Great Bend.

A friend just mailed me a few poems, filled
with crickets and the sap of cicadas,
boats and riverbanks and love, and that is how
you find me. The choice to come here
was a risk, and, it is no mistake.

Our friend is Irish, he's in your last
diary entry: "A late  float. The fishing, fair.
We agreed to repeat this next year."
He sang at your memorial.

You are here nonetheless, beside the Yellowstone
and at the Murray (once the E-lite), where we stayed
a time or two.  I can see the pillow and you, waking,
"I slept so well.  I can't remember when
I slept so well."

The hops are ripe now,
and the sparrows sing in their hedges.

# EPILOGUE

## Watching It Rain

Weeks since the last real storm, here.
A dark afternoon now, shimmering, elegant sheets
of it fall-- or, in corners and stairwells, scintillae—
puddling our numbed, potholed avenues, pouring life
into a parched world stuffed with evils. So dirty.
This rain has no plan. The point is, its plenty.
Other languages may have better words:
Hebrew, *tikkun olam,* to mend a broken world
or, in Japanese, *kintsugi,* the art of joinery,
binding broken pieces together with gold;  the shards
themselves seem golden. I know what I'm seeing now
arriving, liquid and silvery and generous:  Repair.

# ACKNOWLEDGMENTS

Some of these poems appeared in the following publications:
*Cider Press Review, The Comstock Review, Hawai'i Pacific Review, Quiet Diamonds, Rattle Poetry Journal, Sand Hill Review, Santa Clara Review, Still You: Poems of Illness and Healing, The Water-Stone Review, Third Wednesday,* and *Vermont Literary Review.*

A number of poems in this manuscript were published as a chapbook by The Orchard Street Press: *Midnight Exhibition at the Wheatgrass Saloon* (April, 2020).

***

Special thanks to my daughter, Kate Biller, my sister, Ellen Toker, and poet friends, Christine Holland, David Cummings, and the Community of Writers, Tahoe.

As a poet, Elizabeth Chapman was a late bloomer. Although born into a literary family (her parents edited and published *The Writer* magazine and *The Writer's Handbook*), she wrote her first poem at the age of forty-three. She holds academic degrees from Smith College (BA), The Shakespeare Institute, UK (MA), and Columbia University (PhD). A college teacher of English (Renaissance Literature), and, for twenty years, a psychotherapist in private practice, she lives and writes in Palo Alto, California.

Chapman has seen two full-length collections into print: *Candlefish* (University of Arkansas Press, 2004) and *Light Thickens* (Ashland Poetry Press, 2009). She is the author of two chapbooks: *Creekwalker* (MotherTongue Press, 1995) and *Midnight Exhibition at the Wheatgrass Saloon* (The Orchard Street Press, 2020). Since the year 2000, she has been a member of The Community of Writers, Olympic Valley, CA.

## THE WHITE PINE PRESS POETRY PRIZE

Vol. 31 - Our Long Float by Elizabeth Chapman.
Selected by Hélène Cardona.

Vol. 30: *Inquest* by Michael McGriff.
Selected by Gail Wronsky.

Vol. 29: *Easy Victims to the Charitable Deceptions of Nostalgia* by Emily Schulten.
Selected by Marc Vincenz.

Vol. 28: *A Tree Becomes a Room* by J. P. White.
Selected by Danusha Laméris.

Vol. 27: *Blue If Only I Could Tell You* by Richard Tillinghast.
Selected by Joe Wilkins.

Vol. 26: *The Book of Mirrors* by Yun Wang.
Selected by Jennifer Kwon Dobbs.

Vol. 25: *Aflame* by Gary McDowell.
Selected by Sean Thomas Dougherty.

Vol. 24: *Our Age of Anxiety* by Henry Israeli.
Selected by Kathleen McGookey.

Vol. 23: *Secure Your Own Mask* by Shaindel Beers.
Selected by Alan Michael Parker.

Vol. 22: *Bread From a Stranger's Oven* by Janlori Goldman.
Selected by Laure-Anne Bosselaar.

Vol. 21: *The Brighter House* by Kim Garcia.
Selected by Jericho Brown.

Vol. 20: *Some Girls* by Janet McNally.
Selected by Ellen Bass.

Vol. 19: *Risk* by Tim Skeen.
Selected by Gary Young.

Vol. 18: *What Euclid's Third Axiom Neglects to Mention About Circles* by Carolyn Moore.
Selected by Patricia Spears Jones.

Vol. 17: *Notes from the Journey Westward* by Joe Wilkins.
Selected by Samuel Green.

Vol. 16: *Still Life* by Alexander Long.
Selected by Aliki Barnstone.

Vol. 15: *Letters From the Emily Dickinson Room* by Kelli Russell Agodon.
Selected by Carl Dennis.

Vol. 14: *In Advance of All Parting* by Ansie Baird.
Selected by Roo Borson.

Vol. 13: *Ghost Alphabet* by Al Maginnes.
Selected by Peter Johnson.

Vol. 12: *Paper Pavilion* by Jennifer Kwon Dobbs.
Selected by Genie Zeiger.

Vol. 11: *The Trouble with a Short Horse in Montana* by Roy Bentley.
Selected by John Brandi.

Vol. 10: *The Precarious Rhetoric of Angels* by George Looney.
Selected by Nin Andrews.

Vol. 9: *The Burning Point* by Frances Richey.
Selected by Stephen Corey.

Vol. 8: *Watching Cartoons Before Attending A Funeral* by John Surowiecki.
Selected by C.D. Wright.

Vol. 7: *My Father Sings, To My Embarrassment* by Sandra Castillo.
Selected by Cornelius Eady.

Vol. 6: *If Not For These Wrinkles of Darkness* by Stephen Frech.
Selected by Pattiann Rogers.

Vol. 5: *Trouble in History* by David Keller.
Selected by Pablo Medina.

Vol. 4: *Winged Insects* by Joel Long.
Selected by Jane Hirshfield.

Vol. 3: *A Gathering of Mother Tongues* by Jacqueline Joan Johnson.
Selected by Maurice Kenny.

Vol. 2: *Bodily Course* by Deborah Gorlin.
Selected by Mekeel McBride.

Vol. 1: *Zoo & Cathedral* by Nancy Johnson.
Selected by David St. John.